CW01508926

MIND'S EYE:
Notelets & Dial

LAN

Carol Rumens is an ex-Convent-Grammar-School South Londoner.
Having ditched a Philosophy Single Hons. BA for its failure to reveal
the Meaning of Life, she earned a PG Dip. in Writing for the Stage.
Her plays have been performed at Newcastle's Gulbenkian Studio and
London's Soho Poly. *Bezdelki: Small Things* (2018) received a Michael
Marks Best Pamphlet Award, and *Star Whisper* (1983) was shortlisted
for the Dylan Thomas Award. Rumens now lives in North Wales, where
she's a professor emerita of Creative Writing at Bangor University and
writes more-or-less full-time.

Also by Carol Rumens

*Smart Devices: 52 Poems and Commentaries from
the Guardian 'Poem of the Week'* (Carcanet, 2019)

The Mixed Urn (Sheep Meadow Press, 2019)

Perhaps Bag: New and Selected Poems (Sheep Meadow Press, 2017)

Animal People (Seren, 2016)

De Chirico's Threads (Seren, 2010)

Blind Spots (Seren,2008)

Collected Poems, 1968 -2004 (Bloodaxe, 2004)

Plato Park (Chatto (Fiction) 1987, Flamingo, 1988)

Star Whisper (Secker, 1983)

CONTENTS

ISBN: 978-1-916938-54-0

Cover designed by Aaron Kent

Edited and Typeset by Aaron Kent

Broken Sleep Books Ltd
PO BOX 102
Llandysul
SA44 9BG

'The poem is lonely. It is lonely and *en route*. The author stays with it.'

'…But poetry too hurries ahead of us at times. La poésie, elle aussi, brûle nos étapes' ('Poetry, too, skips some stages').

Paul Celan, *The Meridian: Speech on the Occasion of the Award of the Georg Büchner Prize, 1960.*

Mind's Eye

Carol Rumens

Broken Sleep Books

FORENOTE

The poems in this collection are responses to Paul Celan's life and poetics. In honour of the second quotation from the 'Meridian' speech, I have skipped a few stages. The poems in Part 1, Notelets, are short letters to, or about, Celan. They are not chronologically ordered, and only tenuously grounded in biographical realty. Some narratives touch obliquely on actual events, others reveal them in the process of becoming memories or dreams. Some events are fictional, but serve a symbolic purpose.   Part 2 ('Dialogues...') takes the form of conversations between Celan and an imaginary poem of his, un-titled and unfinished, but keeping him company during his last years of mental illness and suicide. Celan's wry humour sometimes seems side-lined by his commentators and translators: when, without my permission, humour surfaced in the dialogue-writing, despite the tragic context, I let it have its way.

There are 3 'free' translations in the collection: Paul Celan's poems 'Notturno' and 'Eis Eden', and Goethe's 'Wandrers Nachtlied'.

Part 1:
NOTELETS

THE CHANGED KEY

In wartime's anytime
there's always a house where someone
should be home but isn't
and a tall child at the door, a faltering key,
an eyeless key-hole. Wartime
makes instant orphans.
Perhaps you punched the window, dropped, terrified
thief into crystal-scattered nowhere
or jerked the back-door handle, cried out
and no-one came hurrying through the kitchen.
There was a smell of cake-tin, opened, emptied.
It sighed *Don't wait. Oh, wait.*
You stood a while, owning nothing,
leaving it. You walked along the platform
and saw the train you'd missed, genocide-wheels
hammering, firing towards you.

STAR

Arc-lights persecuted
the star-holders of Cernăuți all night
but there was always morning, and its sanctioned rays.
The park showed off to every wanderer
luminous greens of yew, viburnum, nettle,
their hungry distance from the mould of tombs.

You cut black petals from the mourning armband
and stitched them to your breast, to hide your *Judenstern;*

and the park-bench was half in shade, and roomy
enough to test the poem — the poem that's with you

wherever you're allowed to take nothing with you.

LABOUR CAMP BREAK-TIME

chuck rock
from hand
to hand
a ring
o'roses
skinned
to bone
who can't
hold rock
keep clawed
is out.

He
who can is permitted a shovel
hides stolen staff-paper
pencils stone posies.

STILLED LONGING

There was a bookstore like a small palace.
Its pinnacles were golden-lit each night
before the synagogue became a glowing-down
of twisted iron and ash, dragging the bookstore with it.

You're not yet afraid.
You swing excitedly inside, you're going
to meet at "German Playwrights", as agreed.

The woman's in a blood-stained shawl, white gloves.
She's standing still. She's reading *Dantons Tod*

with no eyes, no breath to mist the leaves,
mute as the names you struggle to un-mute
in the old young voice you had, the voice which was, they said,
permanently breaking
in den Stimmbruch.

She's not a ghost, she's the tomb of a language
that no-one trusts, that sickens print and speech.

You turn your back. *Du bist die ruh, Mutter*

NIGHT FAIRY-TALE, BUKOVINA, 1941
after 'Notturno'

"Keep your eyes open. Watch
the poplars kick ahead,
bright-booted, like a brigade.
That's Jewish blood in each stitch.

"Bone-clickers pirouette.
One rips the birthing-screen
and whips you out again,
on the tip of a bayonet.

"Run, the wolf-pack's cruising,
the cradle spins on a rod."

I'm scared, Mutti, I'm freezing.
That howl — is it us, or God?

CORONA TO 'CORONA'

Once you had autumn in your palm.
You made a garland of the coronach, twisted
the lovers' twig arms
and falcate leaves into coronation.
The lovers called to God bare-faced, *It's time*
you saw us, God, us lovers,
standing here corona to corona.

Now in the wreathing of years
the word breathes differently —
a virus old as love and new as every
lover's new mutation.

DO NOT RESUSCITATE (2020)

i

Hospitals I know are not
death camps but many
died in their curt selections — hopeless cases
with hopeless little cases
spilled into paint-chipped lockers or
forgotten, never packed:
and the hospitals — hopeless cases
behind grand railings off
the slip-road, scaffolded
in all their blossoming co-morbidities.

We saved their lives, the hopeless hospitals.
We loved them as commanded.
By not being forced to open
their mouths for us, they could afford to feed
oxygen to some, to others, careful letters
advising DNR. (These were 'difficult choices'.)

ii

When movement was forbidden
our retail civilisation
played soldiers... stencilled soles
marched the shopping aisles, right left up down —
loss-maker footfall.
Breathing time, we timed
(faster now we timed)
the coming breathlessness.
We masked, sweated, obeyed
faster, faster, now we learned
the enemy rode on kisses
the better to disable
our currency. We sat in bubbles, watched
the spike-crowned viruses in suits stand firm
on science and obedience and war.

VIENNA

There's no journey that matters
in any story, except
the few rushed steps to the edge of childhood,
the city where you were last seen. It's falling
to other eyes. You're seen
enough to be hated.

What's Vienna, what's Paris
compared to the street beyond dying,
the walking bodily on, the fun of kicking along
the fossil remains of your face?

In the new regime it's official: you, yes, you
are *nimic*. You're not eligible for a visa.
The courtesy of the train,
the waiting room and the ticket man is history.

Did you believe you were different?
Everything's history, haste-story
for the shining only-child
who will limp at last into Paris or Vienna,
smashed and shot but forced to shy at his life.

FLAKES, 2022, 1944

A minute's silence for the dead. Then
you can breathe
the virus-free ash-rich particulate,
say Kaddish, sing Kontakion or simply
groan among friends, take up
smoking again because... you know how it is
because we hear the rumour, Europe's
tank-roll, that Old Normal.

Russia. Snow. Ukraine. Once more you pale
through whirling flakes towards me.
I know I know you, word-ghost never met.
Is your hand too cold...
will you autograph my birth-year?

CHERNIVTSI

'Lonely and en route'
your city like a poem, fugitive,
dawns in and out of tongues.
Call any name, a soot-clump startles down,
pecks at balcony-iron and powdered eggshells, finds
a smear of hope dreamed as the burning trees
dream it, as the terrified blackbirds scream it:
Czernowitz Tshernovits Cernăuți Chernovtsy...
The land of complicated doors
crashes round you. Pick one, it's a temple
with Hebrew's magic migraine on the ceiling,
another, it's the heavy mother-house
of German. You must punch the windows out
and bring in perfect strangers.
After the first fierce eyefuls, they're at home —
even the Russians.

Today, my heart melts, hearing
Mandelshtam's tongue, the rough gold-rich cantata
you loved — still natural, almost neutral.

ANNIVERSARY

It was the year that brought your hundredth birthday.
February had married into flowers,
her canopy, thin straw with a scald of nettles.
I saw your name star-naked
in sunlight, Celandine.

Spring has the shortest breath of any season.
Work-whitened, delicate as ash, the rays
of the barely-born were melting.
Your April deathday fell, you weren't quite fifty
and still the sun-prints travelled, still the petals
remembered and novembered
all that had been golden in your time.

ICE, EDEN
after 'Eis, Eden'

There is a land called Lost, a moon
is flowing in its reeds
and everything once frozen
as we were frozen sees

and warms its power of vision
from two bright earths. The night,
the night, the lye's corrosion
this eye-child brings to light

It sees it sees we're seeing
thou seest and I see
this time of ice, its freeing
from time, its rising free.

PART 2:
DIALOGUES:
a conversation between poet and poem

IN THE ASYLUM

'Art as necessity is very bare'
 you might have been thinking
when Poem interrupted: *Speak, you also —*
you — thin coat I wear
not quite to freeze my balls in No-one's Where.

You flinched. Poem shrugged: *Only an amateur*
would call my type a healer!'

'I'm healed to bloody pieces,' you conceded.
'Pieces are fine!' Poem caught your glance, and stared
into its future critical mass of critics.

By now, you were sweating.
'My God, you, Beyond the Beyond,
Thou of my Thousand Thous,
did all the visionaries really teach you nothing?

God may have an eye, Poem said (an agnostic).
Not yours, not 20-20: not without brightness.
Here, swallow this.

You hurled the empty glass. Poem flew,
a swallow. Rose and sank.
Some other spaceman raced himself to the moon.
You found the harp-string slackened,

the psalm, exhausted.
Books locked their doors. Outside,
ghostly asylum children tried to call
back to a wailing seagull.

PTSD: THE POET'S NIGHTMARE

Moonless raining crystal hurled from the shop
stumbled dash through fire-fall up and into
the hissing house-sized truck
pulled in, parked up, parked right here on the mind-scene's
cries unseen made scene of...
    Cut out the punning, can't you?
        ... mad scene un-ensouling. Blood is glass. My feet keep slipping.
Overcoats sprawled old men bat-naked. *Please calm down.*

Poem and Poet wrestle pointlessly.
Poem sweats, pleads,
Stand still a moment, will you.
Let's prise you free of me.
Time to let go. Ouch, let's go! Move it, b-b-
bastard, or else be handed over
to Commentary Cathedral.
Poet shrinks, jumps into Poem's string-bag.
Poem sighs, somehow shoulders the weight.
If he can't take me
today he can't not take me. I'm his transport.

PONT MIRABEAU: LOST WORDS

Night. Figurehead. Sewage breath. Slimed ledge...

Drink something first, see stars a wandering Siren
a lap a cap a cop a couplet. Style the world again.

Count me out, little Lexical, you know there's no *again*.
No stepping twice into any fluent slop,
however dry and white, no perfect re-run
for us who cherish — what do the quacks call it?
Wiederholungszwang. Repetition compulsion.

That's all a poem is, plus an education.

The deepest, kindest, coldest hug isn't from poem to poet
but hemlock to philosopher. Let me drop.

As if you'd never withered, sun-demented
were never torn without an anaesthetic
as if the cries in Ramah could be tented
as if the light of Zion were prophetic.

SLOWER, STILLER

You held me almost for ever. Poem was tired.
You washed me in gravel, wove me sandals of hair,
and still I'm on the road for you, long word-chain
whose form is homelessness. D'you have a light?
Sometimes I'm followed in the distance by
a kind of blanched shadow. Tell me its name.
It comes and goes in the black-out,
transparent, empty-handed. What does it want?

She. She wants her child.
She'd call him Son. She'd call him God. She'd plead,
'Stroke off my yellow star, my piercing
silenced questions. Pluck the celandine for me'.
You'll never call her closer. Now leave me.

I shall be lonely again, lonelier
than you are, Poem says,
not quite complaining, not quite uncomplaining.
But we have time. Let's steal some syllables
where all is formless, void, the deep of it
leaking dark-water light in the home where no-one's
home, all as it was when death broke through.

You dream the scene again and dream it different.
As always, different.
A yellow-cake-tin-coloured
afternoon (wet April? cold November?)
finds two small glasses and a Bechstein upright,

sheet music pinned between the candle-stubs,
the melody no more than cigarette-smoke
from pianissimo fingers, flickering white
above the keys, the hammers' sticky felt
ticking. And the shadow-
girl who's never there, turns the revolving stool
so she can almost see you, sings in faultless German,
and, with a lion's slow gaze, sings towards you...

'The wind has dropped
asleep, the hills
are silence-steeped,
no forest rustles,
wings are still.
And you? You will,
in this unslept
unrest, know rest'

PAUL CELAN: BRIEF BIOGRAPHY

Paul Celan (1920 - 1970) was born Paul Antschel into a family of German-speaking Jews in Cernăuţi, the capital city of Bukovina. The region at the time was part of Romania. Previously, under Austro-Hungarian rule, Cernăuţi had been known as Czernowitz. Romania's Soviet period was succeeded by the Nazi occupation in 1941.

Paul's education included Hebrew School, at the wish of his Zionist father, Leo. He then undertook pre-medical studies in France, also at his father's persuasion, but in 1939 returned home, and began studying romance philology, continuing to write poetry that was influenced by French surrealism. In the summer of 1942, probably while he was spending the night with friends, his mother and father were seized by the Gestapo and deported to internment camps. He saw neither of them again. The trauma of their sudden disappearance and death was central to his writing. Also crucial was the linguistic dilemma. His mother tongue — and his mother's tongue — were German: to write in the language of his persecutors was essential. He forged a poetic self and style from these breakages, like a master of kintsugi working in words rather than ceramics.

There followed a spell in a labour camp shovelling stones, two years spent in Bucharest, then travel across Europe. Celan spent time in Vienna, went on to settle in Paris, completed his studies and married the artist Gisèle Lestrange. His professional career as poet and translator flourished but anti-Semitic cross-currents in the literary milieu tormented him, and the acclaim eventually won by his work brought no psychic relief. He visited Israel, but rejected emigration: he considered himself one of the last Jews of Europe. He spent time in mental hospitals and found no respite. He drowned himself in April, 1970, by dropping from the Pont Mirabeau into the River Seine.

A more detailed biography may be read here:
https://ciluna27.wordpress.com/2021/11/23/paul-celans-paris/

NOTES

(Most referenced poems are in *The Selected Poems and Prose of Paul Celan*, translated by John Felstiner, (W W Norton, 2001). I have also drawn on some of the information in John Felstiner's invaluable literary biography, *Paul Celan: Poet, Survivor, Jew,* (Yale University Press, 1995.)

1: The Changed Key. Title is based on the poem Mit Wechselndem Schlüssel' / With a Changing Key *(Von Schwelle zu Schwelle/ Threshold to Threshold* 1955).

2: Star. The Judenstern is the Star of David badge that Jews were obliged to wear during Nazi occupation

4: Stilled Longing. The title was suggested by Friedrich Rückert's poem 'Du Bist Die Ruh' (You are Rest and Peace'). *Danton's Death* is the play *Dantons Tod* by Georg Büchner.

7: Night Fairy-Tale, Bukovina, 1941. Variations on Celan's early Surrealist poem, 'Notturno' (*Poems / Die Gedichte*, ed. Barbara Weidemann, Frankfurt/M:Surhkamp, 2018).

8: Corona to 'Corona'. Celan's poem 'Corona' is from *Mohn und Gedächtnis / Poppy and Memory*, 1952. Coronach (Scots & Irish) = funeral lament.

9: Do Not Resuscitate: DNR forms were issued to some elderly patients in UK hospitals during the panic over hospital capacity resulting from the Covid 19 pandemic. Other hospital patients who had lived in care-homes were transported back to their care-homes, despite have caught the virus in hospital and still being infectious.

I0: *Nimic* (Romanian) = nothing.

11: Flakes, 2022, 1944. *Schwarze Flocken / Black Flakes*, is from *Early Poems, 1940 - 1943.* The dates in my title signal the year in which the current war between Russia and Ukraine began, and the year I was born.

12: Chernivtsi. Chernivtsi is the contemporary name of Czernowitz.

13: Anniversary. This Notelet is dated 2020, the year of Celan's 100th centenary.

14: Ice, Eden is a free translation of Eis, Eden from *Die Niemandsrose / The No-One's Rose*, (1963).

PART 2: DIALOGUES: a conversation between poet and poem. The passages spoken by Poem are italicised.

15: "Speak you also"/ Sprich auch du" is the first line of a poem in Celan's collection *Von Schwelle zu Schwelle / From Threshold to Threshold* (1955).

17: Pont Mirabeau: Lost Words. Ramah (Hebrew for 'Height') was a city not far from Jerusalem. When the Babylonians destroyed Jerusalem, the captives were first assembled in Ramah before being taken to Babylon. It was the place where Rachel was heard "weeping for her children and refusing to be comforted, because they are no more. "(Jeremiah 31:15 NIV).

19: 'The wind has dropped...' is a free translation of Goethe's 'Wandrers Nachtlied': I imagine it spoken by Celan's mother Fritzi to her son, both now in a shadow-life beyond death.

ACKNOWLEDGEMENTS

I am very grateful to Helena Nelson and Michael Schmidt for patiently commenting on early drafts of some of these poems. 'Ice, Eden' and 'Wanderer's Night Song' were subsequently published by Michael Schmidt in *PNReview*. In an even earlier form, the embryonic poem-sequence received friendly and heartening encouragement from Stanley Moss, Naomi Foyle and Grace Shulman: it wouldn't have grown without their open-hearted support. I posted versions of a few of the poems on my Guardian blog, Poem of the Week, and would like to thank anyone who commented, or simply 'liked' a poem. It's a small thing, but it's an act of communication, and it matters. Deep thanks to Aaron Kent at Broken Sleep Books for his generous response and commitment in taking on this small collection. And, of course, I owe constant gratitude to Celan's translators who, I suspect, have brought a non-Teutophone as close to the original as it's possible to come. John Felstiner's work has been my constant companion. I gained much, too, from reading Michael Hamburger, who first introduced me to Celan in the early '80s, and from the translations and commentary of Pierre Joris. Finally, love to my favourite teachers, my 2 children and 2 grandchildren, Kelsey, Rebecca, Isabella and Sam, plus a special "thank you" to Becky for some sharp-eyed proofreading. Any mistakes that remain are mine.

LAY OUT YOUR UNREST